Love Your Look

Care & Keeping Advice for Girls

by Mary Richards Beaumont
illustrated by Josée Masse

★ American Girl®

Published by American Girl Publishing

No part of this book may be used or reproduced in any manner whatsoever without written permission except in the case of brief quotations embodied in critical articles and reviews.

21 22 23 24 25 26 27 QP 10 9 8 7 6 5 4 3 2 1

Editorial Development: Barbara Stretchberry
Art Direction and Design: Jessica Rogers
Production: Jessica Bernard, Caryl Boyer, Jodi Knueppel, Cynthia Stiles
Illustrations: Josée Masse
Photos: David Roth
Styling: Deb Ahrens, Sena Rosenberg, T Sammarco, Jolene Schulz
Special thanks to Jamilah Rosemond

This book is not intended to replace the advice of or treatment by physicians or other health-care professionals. It should be considered an additional resource only. Questions and concerns about physical health should always be discussed with a doctor or other health-care professional.

Even though instructions have been tested and results from testing were incorporated into this book, all recommendations and suggestions are made without any guarantees on the part of American Girl. Because of differing tools, materials, ingredients, conditions, and individual skills, the publisher disclaims liability for any injuries, losses, or other damages that may result from using the information in this book. Not all craft materials are tested to the same standards as toy products.

© 2021 American Girl. American Girl and associated trademarks are owned by American Girl, LLC. American Girl ainsi que les marques et designs y afférents appartiennent à American Girl, LLC. MADE IN CHINA. FABRIQUÉ EN CHINE. Retain this address for future reference: American Girl, 8400 Fairway Place, Middleton, WI 53562, U.S.A. Conserver ces informations pour s'y référer en cas de besoin. American Girl Canada, 8400 Fairway Place, Middleton, WI 53562, U.S.A. Manufactured for and imported into the EU by: Mattel Europa B.V., Gondel 1, 1186 MJ Amstelveen, Nederland.

Letter to You

Dear Reader,

You might have noticed that the world does a lot to tell people—especially girls and women—that certain hairstyles, cosmetics, and nail polish make them prettier. But here's what's true: You're just right the way you are. There is *nothing* you need to do to make yourself look any different or more beautiful than the way you look right now. Absolutely nothing.

That doesn't mean, though, that hair and makeup aren't fun. And with some creativity (and parent approval, of course), you can design different looks that showcase your individuality, just as an artist might use paint and a canvas to express herself. This book is packed with ideas and inspiration, plus step-by-step instructions for creating hairstyles, makeup designs, and nail art. You can copy them straight from the book or change them up to create a look that's all your own, as unique as the girl you are.

Your friends at American Girl

Safety first!
Some of the materials and styles in this book require an adult's help. When you see this symbol, be sure to ask an adult to work with you.

Contents

How to Look Like You

Your personal style can help you express who you are.

So, what is style?

When people talk about style, often they mean what clothes you choose, how you wear your hair, or what kind of bookbag you carry. But there's more to it than how you look. Style also includes how you move, how you use your face to communicate, even how you say hello to someone. It's everything you put out into the world.

Of course you've heard the old saying: Don't judge a book by its cover. That means it's important to find out what's inside a person or thing, not simply to decide what you think about it by looking only at the outside. The best way to show people who you are is by using your voice to express how you feel and what you believe. Think of style as the backdrop to your voice, like the scenery in a play that surrounds an actor. The words she says are incredibly important. The costumes and the set and the props? They help tell the story.

7

How Do You Style?

Answer these questions to discover your attitude toward your personal look.

1. Do you have a favorite color?
   a. Yes. And I've loved it forever!
   b. No. My favorite color changes with my mood.

2. How much time does it take you to get dressed and ready for school?
   a. Maybe five minutes. (More time to sleep. Yay!)
   b. It takes a while. I put together outfits and style my hair.

3. What happens when you get your hair cut?
   a. I usually ask for the same style.
   b. I ask for new hairstyles often.

4. What's it like for you when ordering in a restaurant?
   a. Too many choices—so I often order something familiar.
   b. It's easy for me to choose—I love trying new things!

5. Which answer best fits your favorite movie?
   a. I've seen it like *a million* times, so much that I can finish the lines.
   b. I've seen it a lot. Watching movies is so much fun.

Answers

Mostly a's
Tried and True
You know exactly what style you like and what works for you. Experimenting with your look isn't a big thing in your life, which means you have more time to spend on activities you enjoy.

Mostly b's
Up for Anything
You like mixing things up and are eager to try out unexpected combinations to form new looks. Experimenting with your look is fun to you, and you love showing off your new creations.

Chances are, you had answers in both categories. Whatever your attitude toward style, you don't have to change a single thing you're doing. Finding personal style usually comes from trying out different ideas to build something that works. But if a look feels like it fits, then it's the right style for you.

How You Look

Even when you find your style, you'll still have days when you don't feel your best. You might not feel that you look your best, either. That happens to everyone. Often, what you see in the mirror is a reflection of how you feel about yourself rather than how you actually look.

If something's really bothering you, no hairstyle or makeup job can fix it. Talk to a parent or another trusted adult if you're not feeling good about yourself or are struggling with how you look. But styling your hair or applying makeup or nail polish are fun, light activities you can do to brighten your mood and show off your personality. These style details can help people see the whole girl, not just the hairdo or the beauty products. **The point isn't to cover up or to look like someone else—it's to look more like yourself.**

Just as you grow and change, your style can change, too. You may have worn your hair a certain way for a very long time. It probably looks nice. But there's nothing wrong with trying something new. Maybe it's your classic style with a slight change, or maybe it's something completely different. What's important is that it makes you happy and comfortable and confident.

Those feelings are the secret behind any great style. **When you feel good about yourself, it shows.** Confidence always fits perfectly, and it looks really good on you.

Big Important Point
Make style choices to please yourself, not other people. What matters is whether *you* like your style.

Love Your Hair Look

What you do with your hair says something about you.

Styling

There are a lot of reasons that might influence how you wear your hair. You might want to . . .

❋ stay safe or comfortable during an activity.

❋ match an outfit or uniform.

❋ dress up for a special occasion.

❋ celebrate your school or a team.

❋ show off your personality.

❋ honor your culture.

The style you choose shows people a little bit about you. It might say that you're serious, or fun-loving, or athletic. It might signal that you are respectful, or creative, or spirited. It might even say that you're not someone who spends much time worrying about her hair! All those qualities are great. Your hairstyle can help show people your personality without you saying a word.

Most girls have lots of options for styling their hair. And good hairstyles begin with good hair care.

13

Care for Your Hair

Your tresses need TLC, just like the rest of you.

There are about as many different kinds of hair as there are kinds of girls. Hair comes in different colors, textures, and thicknesses. It even grows in different shapes along foreheads. Those unique qualities mean that not every hairstyle in the world can be re-created on every head. It also means that different kinds of hair need different kinds of care.

But some hair-care basics are true for almost everyone. Practicing good habits (and breaking not-so-good ones) is a great first step in having healthy hair.

Do

Handle with care. Use a comb, brush, or pick to gently remove tangles. Instead of rubbing harshly with a towel, pat hair to dry. And go easy on the pulling when using clips or elastics.

Eat well. A nutritious, vitamin-rich diet is as important for your hair as it is for your body. Happy-hair foods include blueberries, yogurt, spinach, lentils, eggs, and avocados.

Be protective. In the daytime, wear a sun hat to shield hair from intense rays. At night, gather hair into a bonnet, scarf, or soft scrunchie—hair doesn't love being mushed on a pillow all night.

Avoid

Twirling   Chewing   Yanking   Scrubbing

All of these no-nos can hurt your hair.

Washing

How often a girl washes her hair depends on the girl. Some girls wash it once a week or less often. Other girls wash every few days or every other day. If you get sweaty on a regular basis, if you use hair styling products, or if your hair tends to feel dirty, you may want to wash every day.

If you have problems with your hair, such as greasiness, breakage, dryness, frizz, or flatness, **it might have to do with how you wash. Time to experiment! Try...**

❋ washing less often if you shampoo daily.
❋ washing more often if you shampoo once in a while.
❋ using less shampoo and conditioner.
❋ switching to a gentler shampoo.
❋ rinsing for longer than usual.

Any of these changes can help fix common hair issues. If you still have trouble, talk to a parent or doctor.

Sometimes hair needs a refresh between shampoos. A quick rinse in the shower (no shampoo) can replace a washing. A spritz of detangling spray can perk up mussed hair. A mist of water can battle bedhead. A dab of styling cream (only enough to make your palms *barely* shiny) slicked over your hair can help tame static or frizz.

Bonus: Hair that has not been freshly washed often holds a style better.

Grooming

Different hair products can help you achieve different styles or help a style last longer. Nobody needs all of them—one or two might do it for you.

Hairspray
Holds hair-styles in place

on dry hair

Gel
Gives strong hold for styling

on damp hair

on damp hair

Mousse
Helps fine or thin hair act thicker

on damp hair

Leave-in conditioner
Reduces breakage and adds moisture

Detangling spray
Eases tangles and adds moisture

on damp or dry hair

Curl cream
Defines curls and tames frizz

on damp hair

Keep in Mind

✳ You can always add more product, but you can't take it away without washing your hair. Too much product can leave hair a major mess! Always start with a tiny bit and build from there.

✳ Follow the directions on the products.

✳ Keep products away from your mouth and eyes.

on damp hair

Edge control
Styles textured baby hairs

CAREFUL!
Have a parent check that your hair products are kid-safe.

Triple Buns

This is a special-looking style that's easy to create.

1. Separate your hair into three equal sections, as if you were going to braid it.

2. Use a hair elastic to make each section into a ponytail.

3. Wrap each ponytail into a bun. Secure with bobby pins.

4. Gently pull on the buns to loosen the hairs and soften the look.

Tip: If you have shorter curly or textured hair, try forming and fluffing the buns instead of pinning them.

Pinned Braids

Make simple braids even prettier with a few extra steps.

1. Make two braids, one by each ear. Secure each with a clear elastic, leaving the tails long.

2. Wrap each braid toward the opposite ear across the back of your head.

3. Use bobby pins to hold the braids in place. Arrange the tails in a pretty way, or tuck them under the braids.

4. Add colorful clips or tuck small flowers into the braids.

Half-Up Topknot

Change up this look by styling the top-knot in different ways.

1. Gather your hair, from your ears up to the top of your head.

2. Coil the hair into a loose bun, securing with bobby pins.

OR, braid the hair. Secure the braid with an elastic and then coil into a bun. Pin.

OR, make a messy loop with the hair and secure with an elastic or scrunchie.

Loopy Faux-Hawk

This wild style is perfect for a school spirit day.

1. Pull the top third of your hair into a high ponytail. Secure with an elastic.

2. Make a loop and secure with a pin or barrette.

3. Repeat with a ponytail at the center back of your head and another at your nape.

4. Use colorful pins or barrettes to secure your bangs or any flyaways as needed.

Hair Color

Your natural hair color is the exact shade it's supposed to be—no need to change it. Still, adding color to your hairstyle can be fun. It gives your look a playful or artsy vibe that can be either barely noticeable or super intense. You can use color all over or to highlight certain parts of your hairstyle. Most kid-safe color doesn't last long, so you can try different looks to figure out your favorite.

A hairstylist in a salon can give you a color treatment. Some color you can do at home. Either way, it's extremely important that you **have an adult help you apply any color.** Hair color is a chemical that can harm you. It can stain your clothing as well as towels, rugs, and surfaces such as floors and countertops. It can even stain your skin. Hair color is a project that requires adult help, every time.

CAREFUL!
Have a parent check that your hair color is kid-safe.

Before you make any decisions about color, know what kind of product you're using.

Color Types

| **Chalk** | **Cream** | **Liquid** | **Spray** |
| Scribbles color onto hair | Slicks color onto hair | Washes color into hair | Mists color onto hair |

A parent can help you decide which hair color product will work best for you. Avoid products made with wax—they can make hair sticky and are difficult to wash out. Apply the product in a room with good air flow (or outside). Make sure that the color doesn't touch your skin or drip into your eyes, and don't inhale any mists or fumes from color treatments.

Color Times

Temporary
This color will last until your next washing. **Note:** It can last longer on (or stain) light-colored hair.

Semipermanent
This color will last through a few washings. It fades over time and eventually disappears.

Permanent
This color is designed to last. It will fade, but you may have to wait until it grows out to be entirely gone. **Note:** Permanent color generally isn't used on kids. But by choosing something that fades away, you can try out more looks!

Keep in Mind

❋ Some school dress codes don't allow hair color. Know the rules.

❋ Hair color will look different depending on the shade of hair you have to begin with. It may show up brightly on lighter hair and look more subtle on darker hair.

❋ Keep hair color products off your skin and away from your mouth and eyes. If you get any on you, rinse it off with water right away and tell a parent.

27

Party in the Front

Frame your face with a pop of color.

1. Cover your clothing. Then gather up some of the hair around your face.

2. Put the remaining hair into a ponytail or clip to keep it out of the way. Adjust the amount of loose hair until it's the amount you want colored.

3. Ask an adult to apply color to the selected hair in the front.

4. Wait for the color to set or dry, and then let the rest loose.

Rockin' Braids

Carefully placed color stripes make braids look extra cool.

1. Cover your clothing. Make one or more braids on one or both sides of your head.

2. Put the remaining hair into a ponytail or clip to keep it out of the way.

3. Ask an adult to apply color to each braid. If you're using spray, hold a piece of paper between the braids to avoid overlapping color.

4. When the color is set or dry, let down the ponytail and tease the unbraided hair to create volume. Use hairspray to hold hair in place.

Candy Tips

Streaks of color on the ends of your hair are like sprinkles on a cupcake!

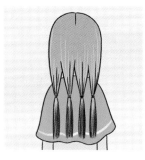

1. Cover your clothing. Then divide hair into four sections.

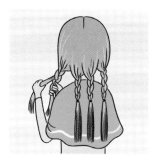

2. Braid each section and secure with elastics, leaving the tails long.

3. Ask an adult to apply different colors to the braids' tails.

4. When the colors are set or dry, let the braids loose.

Love Your Makeup Look

A touch of color on your face
can enhance your features.

You do not need makeup.

Commercials, magazines, and other media send messages telling girls and women that cosmetics will make them look prettier or more professional, or that they should use makeup to cover up or to make themselves look different. But it's worth saying again: **You don't need it.**

That doesn't mean that you can't enjoy makeup. A makeup look can be a nice accessory to an outfit, especially on a special occasion or day of celebration. It's fun to use your face as a canvas, artfully applying different colors and shading to make parts of your face stand out. A makeup look can be part of your style.

35

Why Makeup?

Cosmetics are products such as liquids, creams, powders, and gels designed to be applied to the face to enhance how it looks. Makeup works by adding or removing contrast. It makes eyelashes look darker or stand out more. It helps lips or cheeks seem rosier. It can give skin a more even tone—making it look like the same color all over—and can hide blemishes or other spots. It can be used to create looks that appear natural or bold looks that stand out.

Many girls do not wear makeup at all or use it only on certain occasions. Parents generally have opinions about whether makeup is right for their kids, so it's best to have a conversation with a parent if you think you're ready to try it.

You might want to try makeup if you're . . .

* attending a special event, such as a wedding.
* going to a big game or concert and you want to look festive.
* hanging out with friends and want to experiment with different looks.

You might want to avoid makeup if you're . . .

* exercising.
* swimming.
* doing sports.
* playing outside.

Why? Most makeup will run or wipe right off when your face is sweaty or wet.

Stage Makeup

Many performances—such as dance recitals, gymnastics meets, and plays or musicals—include makeup as part of the costume or uniform. These are exaggerated looks designed to help your face be seen from very far away and under bright lights. This kind of makeup is a lot different from everyday makeup.

CAREFUL!
Have a parent check that your makeup is kid-appropriate.

37

Makeup Basics

You probably have seen aisles upon aisles of cosmetics at discount stores. In malls, there are entire shops devoted to beauty products and huge counters full of makeup in department stores. Many colors. Many types. Many different choices.

What does all that stuff do?

Lips

Lipstick
Slicks on solid, creamy color

Lip gloss
Paints on sheer, gel-like color

Tinted lip balm
Slicks on sheer, moisturizing color

Lip liner
Draws on to define your lips' edges

Eyes

Mascara
Combs on to make eyelashes look darker, longer, or thicker

Eyeliner
Frames the eyes with color that is drawn or painted along the lashes

Eye shadow
Brushes or smears on color and shading to eyelids

Cover Up
Like art supplies, makeup can stain clothing and surfaces. It's a good idea to wear an art smock to protect your clothes and lay down paper or an old cloth to collect any drips or spills.

Face

Foundation
Smears on to even out skin tone

Powder
Brushes on to reduce shine

Concealer
Dabs on to cover spots

Tinted moisturizer
Slicks on sheer, moisturizing color

Blush
Adds a flushed look to cheeks

Eyebrow makeup
Gives brows shape and solid color

What Does the Label Mean?

Beyond the product color, makeup packaging contains lots of descriptive words. Here's what some of them mean:

noncomedogenic: designed to not clog your skin's pores and cause breakouts

natural: may contain fewer harmful chemicals than other products (or no harmful chemicals at all)

hypoallergenic: may produce fewer allergic reactions than other products

cruelty-free: finished product is not tested on animals to be sure it's safe

Labels also list the product's ingredients. Work with a parent to research specific ingredients to avoid, and then make sure the makeup you use doesn't contain them.

Makeup Safety

Learning to use makeup properly and safely is important. Beauty counters and stores often have workers who can show you the right way to apply makeup. A parent or other trusted adult might have good tips, too. Or ask a parent if you can watch tutorial videos online.

Stay-Safe Rules

❖ **Be especially careful around your eyes.** There's a risk of poking or injuring your eyes when using eye makeup. Applying it requires care and focus. Use a mirror. Take your time.

❖ **Know what you're putting on your lips.** Any lip product gets wiped or smeared away over time. But some of it ends up inside your mouth when you speak, drink, eat, or lick your lips. So be sure that your lip products are fresh and safe.

❖ **Watch for allergic reactions.** Some makeup can cause problems, especially if you are sensitive. If any makeup product ever makes your skin or eyes burn, itch, puff up, or turn red, use makeup remover or soap to wash it off right away and tell a parent.

❖ **Always wash your face.** Never go to sleep wearing makeup—it can cause breakouts or infections. Wash your face with a gentle cleanser. Use makeup remover to gently wipe away everything the soap missed, especially around your eyes.

Makeup has an expiration date. It can dry out and not work anymore, or it can grow bacteria over time. It's important to throw away makeup after it has expired, even if you haven't used it all. When you first use a product, write the date on it with a permanent marker. Then start counting forward from that date.

3 months	1 year	2 years
Mascara, liquid eyeliner	Most other makeup	Pencil eyeliner, powder, blush

Keep in Mind

* Sharing is kind, but not when it comes to makeup. Cosmetics get super germy. Using another person's makeup can irritate your skin or eyes. It can even make you really sick. Keep your makeup to yourself.

* To keep germs away, wash makeup brushes with a gentle shampoo after each use.

* If you visit a store that offers makeup to test, never apply it directly to your face or touch the actual product with your fingers or lips. Use disposable applicators to try out products on the back of your hand or on your forearm; then wash them off.

Big Day Out

This light, natural makeup look is a fun accent to a dressy outfit.

1. Wash and dry your face.

2. Apply a light layer of mascara to your top eyelashes. Let dry.

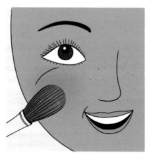

3. Add a light layer of blush to your cheeks, on the fleshy "apples" that pop up when you smile.

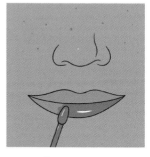

4. Put on lip gloss that is clear or a color just a shade darker than your natural lip color.

Tip: Keep tissues handy. They are great for blotting makeup if you've goofed or put on too much.

Go for It!

Try a superhero-like style for a fun event such as a concert or dance.

1. Wash and dry your face.

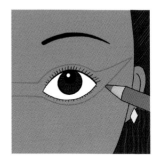

2. Use a pencil eyeliner (in whatever color you like) to draw a big swoopy shape around both eyes, from temple to temple.

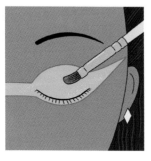

3. Use brightly colored cream eyeshadow to fill in the shape. A lip brush can be helpful for making tiny strokes at the edges.

4. Finish with a dusting of powder to help set the makeup.

Spirit, Let's Hear It

Wear your school colors proudly with this eye-catching look.

1. Wash and dry your face.

2. Color the inner halves of your eyelids with cream or powder eyeshadow in a school color.

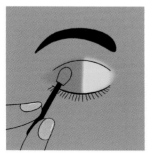

3. Color the outer halves of your lids with another school color.

4. If desired, continue the outer color in a slim triangle curving from your eye toward the end of your eyebrow. (This technique is called a "cat eye.")

Love Your Nail Look

Show off pops of color and cute designs on your fingers.

You use your hands for so many different things, and they are constantly in motion. Because you see them all the time, an uplifting shade, a creative design, or an adorable little shape painted on your nails can brighten your mood instantly. And just as hair and makeup can help you express your style, nail polish and nail art can highlight your individuality and add an extra detail to an outfit.

Many girls do not wear nail polish at all or use it only on certain occasions. Parents generally have opinions about whether nail polish is right for their kids, so it's best to have a conversation with a parent if you think you're ready to try it.

Learning to polish your own nails takes time, especially since you'll have to get used to working with the hand you don't write with. But as you build confidence and skill, you can add details, such as shapes or patterns, to your look. An extra set of hands from a parent or friend can really help at first.

Nail Basics

Nail polish looks start with healthy, groomed nails.

The number one rule about your hands: You've got to wash them. A lot. Clean hands are essential to your overall health, since germs from your hands can easily transfer to your eyes, nose, or mouth. If you're washing your hands often enough and for long enough (at least 20 seconds with lots of soap and water), your hands and fingernails can get very dry.

So in addition to washing, it's important to moisturize. Moisturizing your hands . . .

❄ keeps skin from becoming itchy or cracked.

❄ prevents painful hangnails.

❄ strengthens nails.

Use moisturizer on your hands and nails at least once a day. You'll also need to pay special attention to your fingernails.

A nail-care routine is easy to do on your own.

1. Brush. Use a nail brush with soap and water to thoroughly clean underneath the tip of each nail.

2. Trim. Use a nail clipper to carefully shorten and shape your nails.

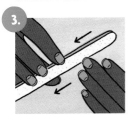

3. File. Use a nail file to smooth out any sharp edges. File by gently scraping in only one direction. Sawing back and forth can shred your nails.

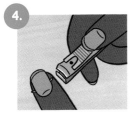

4. Clip. Use a nail clipper to snip off any hangnails. Never pull or bite off hang-nails. That could rip the skin (ouch!) or cause an infection (gross!).

5. Soothe. Rub a rich moisturizer into the fronts and backs of your hands as well as into each nail and cuticle.

Performing this routine at least once a week will keep your nails neat and healthy—and make a perfect canvas for a nail polish look.

Nail Polish Safety

Some nail polishes contain harmful chemicals. The good news is, there are brands of polish without those ingredients, so they're better for kids. Still, it's important to involve a parent in any decisions about using chemical products and to make sure that you have permission.

Stay-Safe Rules

✲ **Use nontoxic polish, always.** Safer polishes will have labels marked with numbers that mean the polish does not contain that number of the scariest ingredients. Polishes marked 7-free or higher are your best bet.

✲ **Treat nail polish as you would art paint.** That means always protecting clothing, floors, furniture, and other surfaces while using it. Keep it away from younger siblings and pets.

✲ **Quit your nail-biting habit, if you have one.** It's not safe to swallow the little bits of polish that would come off in your mouth when you chew your nails.

✲ **Be careful around food.** If you're making something in the kitchen—such as forming cookies with your hands—know that polish can come off and get into the food. Remove your polish and wash your hands before you start cooking.

Is My Nail Polish Expired?

If bottled nail polish has separated into layers, that doesn't mean it's gone bad. Ask a parent to add a few drops of nail polish thinner (or polish remover) to the bottle; then roll it between your palms to mix. But do throw out polish if it:

✲ Seems globby, crumbly, or stringy
✲ Doesn't mix well after you've added thinner
✲ Is more than two years old

Removing Polish

Most nail polish removers are chemicals that dissolve polish so that you can wipe it away. Nail polish remover is stinky, and the fumes can hurt your lungs and sting your eyes. So it's important to be careful with it. Work with a parent to choose the remover that's right for you, and get adult help when removing polish.

To remove polish:

1. Find a room with good air flow. Cover your work surface.

2. Soak a cotton ball with remover, and press the soaked ball to each nail to let the remover start working.

3. Use the cotton ball to rub polish away. Add more remover or start a fresh cotton ball, if needed.

4. Use a cotton swab dipped in remover to get at polish near cuticles, if needed.

Glittery nail polishes can be super stubborn. Press a cotton ball soaked with remover to the nail for a few seconds to loosen the sparkles.

Peeling Polish
It's important to use remover to take off old polish. Peeling or picking it off can damage the top layer of your nails, making them weaker and more likely to break.

CAREFUL!
Have a parent check that your polish and polish remover are kid-safe.

53

How to Polish

Taking your time will help your polish
job look great and last longer.

1. Find a room with good air flow, and cover your work
surface and clothing.

2. Groom your nails using the directions on page 51, but
don't apply moisturizer. Polish covers better when nails
are clean and dry.

3. With the cap still on, roll the nail polish bottle between
your palms. Don't shake it—that can add air bubbles to
the polish, which can cause bumps on your nails.

4. Open the bottle. Carefully wipe excess polish from the
brush against the inside of the bottle's opening, leaving
only enough polish on the brush to paint one nail.

5. Start by painting the nails on the hand you write with.
(That way, your less-sure hand won't have wet, smudgeable
polish on it.)

6. Paint your pinky first, placing the brush at your cuticle and
gliding up toward the top of the nail. Apply three stripes
in this order: middle, outer edge, inner edge.

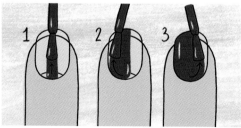

Add just enough polish to coat the nail. Too little, and
you'll have gaps. Too much, and the polish will get messy.
Take care to get polish right up to the edge of the nail
without hitting skin. Be patient: This all takes practice!

7. Repeat on your other fingers, doing your thumb last. Your thumb will probably need more brushstrokes than other nails, because it's bigger. Then repeat on the other hand.

8. Let dry. Drying takes at least several minutes, longer if the polish layer is thick. It's best to let polish set for 30 minutes or more, taking care not to smudge.

9. Use a cotton swab dipped in remover to carefully wipe away any stray polish on surrounding skin.

Do Your Toes Too!

You can follow the same steps for painting your toenails. Wait at least two hours before putting on shoes or socks. Sandals are OK sooner. (**Note:** Always clip toenails straight across.)

Keep in Mind

❋ Adding a second coat of polish deepens the color. Be sure the first coat is dry before adding a second.

❋ Basecoats (under the color) and topcoats (over the color) are clear polishes designed to make polish last longer and prevent chipping. If add either of these steps, allow plenty of drying time between coats.

❋ A tiny smudge might be disguised with a second coat. A major smudge will likely require repainting. Remove smudged polish with a cotton swab dipped in remover, taking care not to let it touch your other polished nails. Then reapply polish.

Nail Designs

Combine different polishes into eye-catching designs.

Glitter Glam

Polish nails and let dry. Then carefully apply a coat of glittery polish over each nail to create a colorful, layered look.

Ombre

Use a light polish color to paint a nail close to the cuticle. Let dry. Follow with a darker color in the middle of the nail, and an even darker color at the tip.

Rainbow Range
Paint different nails in different colors. You can make hands match or add color randomly. Or paint just one nail on each hand a different color.

Confetti
Polish nails, and let dry. Dip a toothpick into a bottle of nail polish that's a different color, and dot the color onto the nails. Repeat with as many dots and colors as you like.

Tip: Add art to every nail, or just a few, or just one—whatever fits your style.

Nail Patterns

Simple tools can help you create cool nail art.

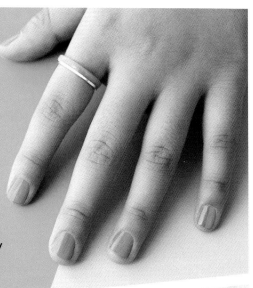

Half and Half
Cut a strip of washi or masking tape and apply it to half of an already polished and dry nail, pressing down to seal the edges. Polish the exposed half of the nail with a new color. Let the new polish dry, and then carefully peel off the tape.

Stencils
You can purchase nail stencils to help you make different shapes or patterns such as scallops, zigzags, and waves.

Toothpick Shapes

Use a toothpick to drop a big dot of contrasting polish onto dry polish. Then drag star-like points out from the center to make a sunburst. For a heart, drop two smaller dots of polish next to each other onto dry polish. Then drag the dots to meet in a single point below. Finish with a coat of clear polish.

Color Blocks

Cut thin strips of masking tape or washi tape. Apply the strips in a pattern to nails that are polished and dry, pressing down to seal the edges. Add contrasting polish between the strips to form color blocks. Let the new polish dry, and then carefully peel off the tape. Finish with a coat of clear polish.

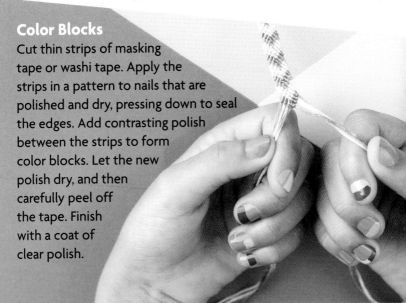

Nail Stickers

Start with a base of clear or colorful polish; then add stickers for extra flair.

Tape Pattern

Use scissors to cut a piece of colorful washi tape to cover a nail. Press the tape onto a dry nail, smoothing out bumps and making sure it is sealed tightly on all edges. Cover with two coats of clear polish, letting it dry between coats.

Tape Stripes

Cut a thin strip of colorful washi tape and press it onto dry polish, smoothing out bumps and pressing down to seal the edges. Cover with two coats of clear polish, letting it dry between coats.

Tape Shapes

Use a paper punch to create a shape in a piece of washi tape. Place the shape carefully onto an already polished and dry nail, smoothing out bumps and pressing down to seal the edges. Cover with a coat of clear polish. Let dry.

Stickers

You can purchase nail stickers in all sorts of shapes and designs. Place stickers carefully onto dry polish, smoothing out bumps and sealing the edges. Cover with a coat of clear polish. Let dry.

Tip: Stickers are great for covering up polish smudges.

CAREFUL!

Have a parent check that your stickers are made for nails.

Love the Whole You

When you look in the mirror, it's important that you like what you see. Be sure to look beyond any makeup or hairstyle to examine your eyes and your smile. See that glow? That's your kindness, your determination, your creativity, your bravery, your empathy. Makeup, nail polish, and hairdos have got nothing on those qualities, which are the best beauty makers in the world. So stock up!

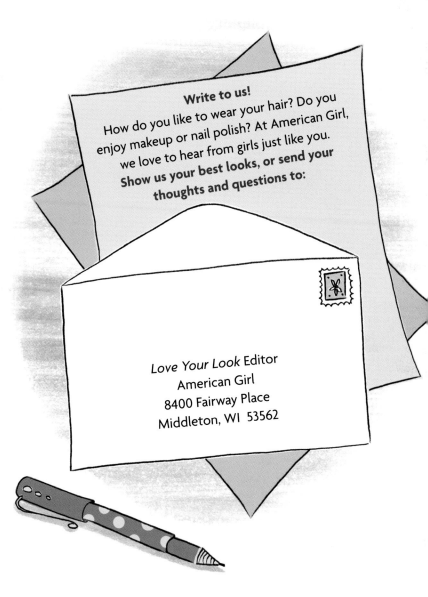

Write to us!

How do you like to wear your hair? Do you enjoy makeup or nail polish? At American Girl, we love to hear from girls just like you. Show us your best looks, or send your thoughts and questions to:

Love Your Look Editor
American Girl
8400 Fairway Place
Middleton, WI 53562

(All comments and suggestions received by American Girl may be used without compensation or acknowledgment. Sorry, photos cannot be returned.)

Here are some other American Girl books you might like:

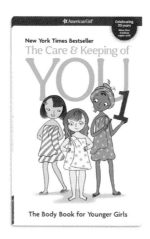

Each sold separately. Find more books online at americangirl.com.

Parents, request a FREE catalog at **americangirl.com/catalog**.
Sign up at **americangirl.com/email** to receive the latest news and exclusive offers.

Discover online games, quizzes, activities,
and more at **americangirl.com/play**